Brilliant Support Activities

Understanding Materials

Alan Jones, Roy Purnell and Janet O'Neill

Brilliant Publications

We hope you and your class enjoy using this book. Other books in the series include:

Understanding Living Things   1 897675 59 3
Understanding Physical Processes   1 897675 61 5

Published by Brilliant Publications,
The Old School Yard, Leighton Road,
Northall, Dunstable, Bedfordshire LU6 2HA

Written by Alan Jones, Roy Purnell and Janet O'Neill

Designed and illustrated by Small World Design

The authors are grateful to the staff and pupils of
Gellideg Junior School, Merthyr Tydfil for their help.

Printed in Spain by E.G. Zure. 48950 – Erandio (Bizkaia)

First Published in 2000
ISBN 1 897675 60 7

Contents

	Link to NC	page
Introduction to the series		4
Introduction to the book		5
Natural or made	1a	6
Groupings	1a	7
Made of what?	1a	8
Water or not?	1a, 1e	9
See-through properties	1a	10
Gases	1e	11
Liquids other than water	1e, 2d	12
Solids	1a, 1e	13
Float or sink?	1a	14
Fizzy drinks	1e, 2a, 3b	15
Ice and water	1a, 1e	16
Melting	1b, 2c, 2d	17
Burning wood	2c, 2f	18
Barbecue heat	1b	19
Stick to magnets	1a	20
Rusting	1a, 2c, 2f	21
Dissolving	2a, 2d, 3b	22
Investigating dissolving	2a, 2d, 3b	23
Drinking chocolate	2a, 3d, 3b	24
What happens to the Smarties?	2a, 2d, 3e	25
Tea bags	2a, 3b, 3c	26
Filtering	2a, 3b, 3c	27
Changes	2c, 2f	28
Heating bread	2c, 2f	29
Changes to a flame	2c, 2f	30
What is changing?	2c, 2e	31
Burning a candle	2c, 2f	32
What is in the bubbles?	1e	33
What is needed?	1a	34
Compost	1a, 2c	35
Water cycle	2d	36
What happens?	2a, 3e, 2e	37
Snowman	1a, 1b, 2c	38
Jelly and plaster	1a, 1d	39
The lost ring	1a, 3a	40
How much will dissolve?	3e	41
Concrete	1d, 2a, 2c	42
Hot and cold	2c	43
Gases in liquids	2c	44
Problem solving, 1		45
Problem solving, 2		46
Problem solving, 3		47
Problem solving, 4		48

Introduction to the series

This series is designed to help the slower learner or pupils with learning difficulties at Key Stage 1 and 2 develop the essential skills of observation, predicting, recording and drawing conclusions. These pupils often have been neglected in more conventional commercial schemes of work. The books contain a mixture of paper-based tasks and 'hands on' activities. Symbols have been used to indicate different types of activities:

  What to do

  Think and do

  Read

  Investigate

The sheets support the attainment target for Key Stage 2 Science, Section 1: Scientific enquiry and Section 3: Materials and their properties. The practical investigations use materials readily available in most primary schools. The activities have been vetted for safety, but as with any classroom based activity, it is the responsibility of the class teacher to do a risk assessment with her/his own pupils in mind.

The sheets usually introduce one concept or National Curriculum statement per sheet (unless they are review sheets). The sheets are designed for use by individual pupils or to be used as a class activity if all the class are working at the same ability range. They can be used in any order, so that you can choose the sheet that best matches a pupil's needs at that particular time. As with any published activities, the sheets can be modified for use by specific pupils or groups. The sheets can be used as a support for your present schemes, as an assessment task, or even as a homework task. If used for assessment purposes then you will need to devise a marking scheme or level indicator. Generally the sheets are designed for use with levels 1–3 but some can be used at level 4.

The sheets use simple language and clear, black line illustrations to make them easy to read and understand. They have been tested to check that they can be understood by pupils with learning difficulties. Although the sheets have a reduced vocabulary, they encourage pupils to produce written responses and to develop their writing skills.

No particular reference has been made to any type of disability as the activities should be accessible to a wide range of pupils and it is up to the teacher to select the most suitable modes of access to match the needs of their pupils. For example, the activities could be photo-enlarged, converted to raised tactile diagrams, or recorded on an audio tape.

Introduction to the book

The topics in this book help pupils understand the properties of materials through investigation. They reinforce methods of scientific enquiry by requiring pupils to plan, carry out practical activities, consider evidence, and present ideas and conclusions. They focus on grouping and classifying materials, changing materials, and separating mixtures of materials, but other concepts such as forces, heat and magnetism are also included within the context of understanding the properties of materials.

The worksheets in this book overlap and you will find that several statements of the National Curriculum are covered several times in a number of different ways. This is to allow you to use the worksheets to repeat work on particular concepts to reinforce the pupils' learning. However the worksheets are not designed to be used in any particular sequence. They are not a teaching scheme, but are a resource which you can use to enrich or augment your own particular scheme of work according to the needs of your pupils.

Some worksheets encourage an open ended response, others are designed to lead pupils to a particular answer. Some start with easy tasks and progress to more difficult extension activities which we have called 'Think and do'. Others are at one level of difficulty. The variety is designed to give the worksheets flexibility and to allow you to select the most appropriate worksheet for your pupils.

The answers to the problem solving sheets are as follows:

page 45
- The sailor can use the Sun to evaporate the water from salt water by turning it into water vapour. If he had hung a bottle of cold sea water over the salt water, the water vapour would condense on the outside as droplets of pure water.
- The farmer should use a filter.
- The engineer should use a magnet to see if it is attracted to the wall.

page 46
- a) Warming the water will cause the water level to rise.
  b) Cooling the water will cause the water level to fall.
- As the wire is heated it expands and the pointer goes up.
- a) Temperature.
  b) Calibrate the scales using known temperatures.

page 47
- The candle uses up oxygen when it burns. The candle stops burning when all the oxygen is used up.
- The water level will remain the same. The ice contracts when it melts (water expands when it freezes – this is why ice floats), but some of the ice cube was above the water level.
- The balance will remain the same because the ice does not change in weight when it melts.

page 48
- Rusting will not occur unless there is both moisture and oxygen (air) present.
- The droplets of water are caused when moisture in the air condenses on the cold window.
- a) A combination of moisture and air causing a chemical change to the iron gate.
  b) Probably a combination of acid rain causing a chemical change to the limestone and erosion by ice, wind and rain.

Natural or made?

What to do

Draw a ring round **N** if the materials are natural.

Draw a ring round **M** if the materials are made by people.

 N   M

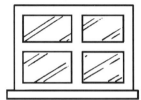 N   M

 N   M

 N   M

 N   M

Think and do

A cat is natural because ...

. . . .

. . . .

. . . .

Groupings

Read

There are thousands of materials in nature and even more manufactured ones.

What to do

Choose the correct words to write on each line:

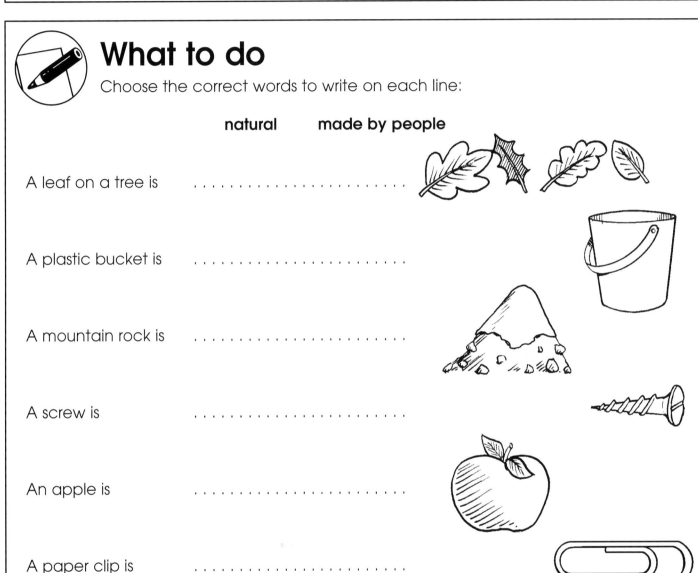

	natural	made by people
A leaf on a tree is	. . . .	
A plastic bucket is	. . . .	
A mountain rock is	. . . .	
A screw is	. . . .	
An apple is	. . . .	
A paper clip is	. . . .	

Think and do

Choose the correct word to finish the sentence:

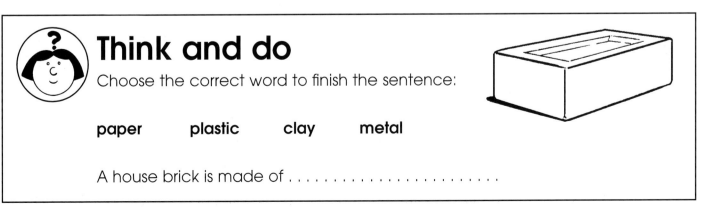

paper   plastic   clay   metal

A house brick is made of . . . .

Made of what?

What to do

Draw a line from the material to the thing made of that material.

Metal

Brick

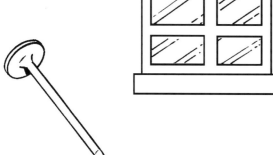

Paper

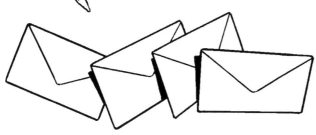

China

Glass

Think and do

Which thing came from the wood of a tree? . . . .

Are any of the things alive? . . . .

What is glass made from? . . . .

Water or not?

 ## What to do

Choose the correct word to write on each line:

ice   **water**   **steam**

Rain is . . . .

A boiling kettle gives out . . . .

Snow is . . . .

An **iceberg** is . . . .

The cold drink has . . . . and . . . . in it.

 ## Think and do

Water can be turned into ice by . . . .

Water can be turned into steam by . . . .

See-through properties

 ## What to do

Do these things let light through? Draw a ring round **Yes** or **No**.

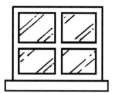 Glass of a window **Yes** **No**

 Brick wall **Yes** **No**

 Water **Yes** **No**

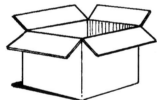 Cardboard **Yes** **No**

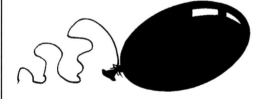 Balloon **Yes** **No**

Think and do

The window lets light through. We say it is: **t** _ _ _ _ _ _ _ _ _ _

Cut out the letters and rearrange them to find the word.

r	a	n	s	t	t
r	a	n	e	p	

Gases

What to do

Write the correct word below each picture to show which gas is in the following things:

air   steam   carbon dioxide

Cola

. . . .

Bubbles in a fish tank

. . . .

A boiling kettle

. . . .

A balloon

. . . .

An underwater diver

. . . .

A fire extinguisher

. . . .

Cooling towers at a power station

. . . .

Think and do

What gases do you breathe in?   . . . .

What gases do you breathe out?   . . . .

Liquids other than water

Read

Water, oil and washing-up liquid are all liquids.

Investigate

Try this:

Add 3 drops of washing-up liquid. Stir.

Plastic cup ——→

Water ——→

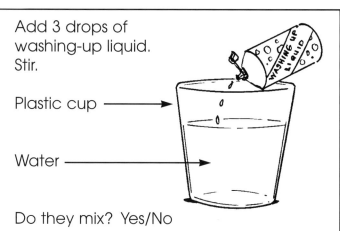

Do they mix? Yes/No

Add 3 drops of cooking oil. Stir.

Plastic cup ——→

Water ——→

Do they mix? Yes/No

Draw or write what happens now.

3 drops of each

Plastic cup ——→

Water ——→

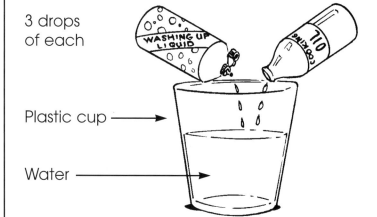

Think and do

Do these liquids have water in them? Write **Yes** or **No**.

Cooking oil . . . .   Cola   . . . .

Cup of tea   . . . .      Petrol   . . . .

Solids

Read

A **solid** has its own shape. A piece of wood or an iron nail is a solid.
A **liquid** needs a container, such as a bottle, to hold it in.

What to do

Choose the correct word to finish each sentence:

solid   liquid

Ice cubes are . . . .

Water is a . . . .

A block of soap is a . . . .

A loaf of bread is a . . . .

Cooking oil is a . . . .

Think and do

When a piece of wood is sawn up,

it is a . . . .

because . . . .

. . . .

Float or sink?

What to do

Write whether you think each thing will **float** or **sink** in water.

Ice will . . . .

A paper clip will . . . .

A coin will . . . .

A matchstick will . . . .

An iron nail will . . . .

An apple will . . . .

A full can of cola will . . . .

An empty can of cola will . . . .

You can investigate this if you wish.

Think and do

A heavy metal boat will float because . . . .

. . . .

. . . .

Fizzy drinks

Read

All fizzy drinks contain the gas carbon dioxide.

What to do

Look at a glass of clear lemonade. Answer these questions.

Where are the bubbles?

. . . .

Draw them.

Are all the bubbles the same size?

. . . .

What happens to the bubbles when they reach the top?

. . . .

. . . .

Think and do

What would happen to a currant or raisin if you added it to the lemonade?

If you do the experiment, remember to record all you see.

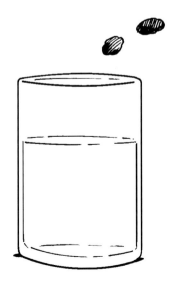

Arm bands help you to float in a swimming pool

because . . . .

. . . .

. . . .

Ice and water

Investigate

Take a coloured ice cube or piece of iced lolly and add it to water. Do not stir. Watch and draw what happens.

Think and do

Try again using warm water. Draw what happens.

I think this happens because . . . .

. . . .

. . . .

Melting

 ## Read

It is a hot day and Sally's ice cream begins to melt in the sun.

 ## What to do

What could Sally do to stop the ice cream from melting so fast?

. . . .

. . . .

. . . .

Think and do

Why doesn't ice cream melt when inside the freezer in the shop?

. . . .

. . . .

What material would be good to wrap a carton of ice cream in to carry it home?

. . . .

. . . .

Name some things that should be kept in a fridge or freezer to stop them melting.

. . . .

. . . .

Burning wood

Read

This is a barbecue.

The fuel was wood.

Sausages were cooked.

What to do

Explain what changed during the barbecue.

The wood changed to . . . .

. . . .

The pink sausages . . . .

. . . .

Think and do

Where did the smells come from?

. . . .

. . . .

. . . .

Barbecue heat

 ## Read

This is a barbecue.

The fuel was wood and it got very hot.

The sausages grilled well.

 ## What to do

Why did the cook use a long metal fork with a wooden handle?

. . . .

. . . .

What happens if the sausages are left on the barbecue too long?

. . . .

. . . .

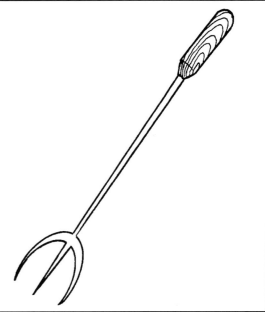

 ## Think and do

This sausage is inside a bun.

Will it burn your fingers? . . . .

. . . .

Two materials that are good heat insulators are . . . .

and . . . .

What other things could be barbecued? . . . .

. . . .

Stick to magnets

What to do

Put a tick ✓ in the box next to the things you think a magnet would 'stick' to.

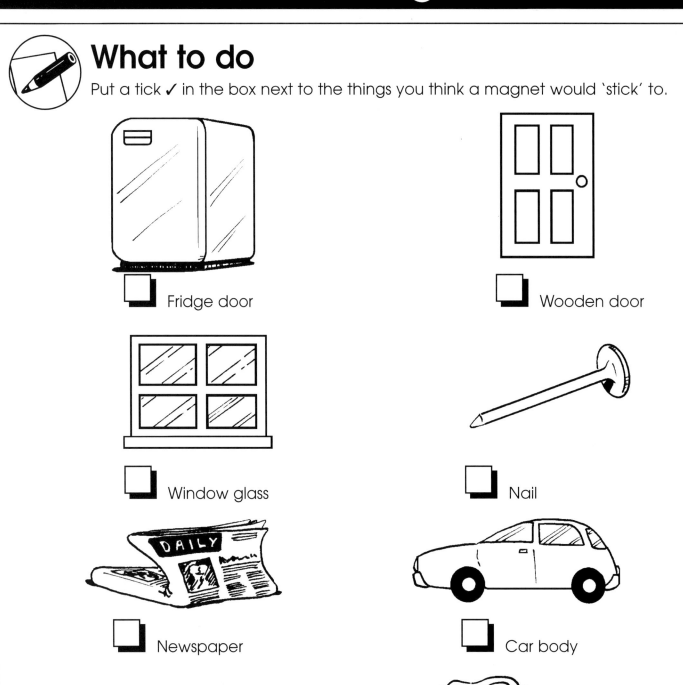

⬜ Fridge door

⬜ Wooden door

⬜ Window glass

⬜ Nail

⬜ Newspaper

⬜ Car body

⬜ Plastic bag

You can investigate this if you wish.

Think and do

Do you think a magnet will stick to a drinks can?

Try it and see.

Rusting

Read

Rusting happens when things made of iron are left out in the air and rain.

What to do

Put a tick ✓ in the box by the things that you think will rust.

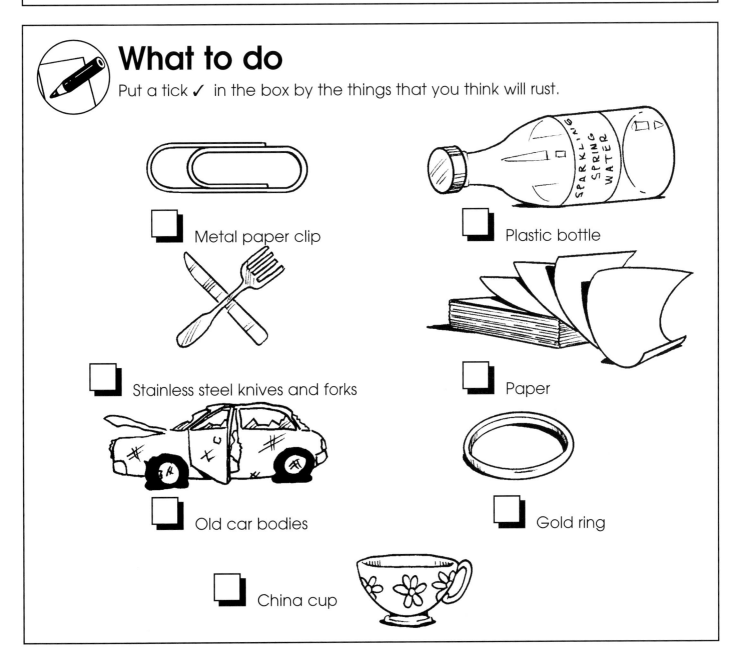

☐ Metal paper clip

☐ Plastic bottle

☐ Stainless steel knives and forks

☐ Paper

☐ Old car bodies

☐ Gold ring

☐ China cup

Think and do

What can be done to stop or slow down rusting?
Write or draw your answer.

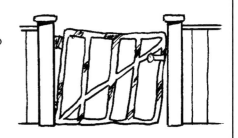

Dissolving

Read

Some things are **soluble**. This means they dissolve in water.
Other things are **insoluble**. They do not dissolve in water.

What to do

Put a tick ✓ in the box to show which things are **soluble** and which things are **insoluble**.

	Soluble	Insoluble
Sugar is	☐	☐
Coffee is	☐	☐
Hair is	☐	☐
Bread is	☐	☐
Margarine is	☐	☐
Orange juice is	☐	☐
Glass is	☐	☐
Skin is	☐	☐

You can investigate this if you wish.

Think and do

Does salt dissolve better in warm water or in cold water?

Try it and see.

Investigating dissolving

Investigate

Add one spoonful of white sugar to a glass of water.
Write or draw what happens.

White sugar

Is there a difference between how brown and white sugar
dissolve in water?   Yes/No

White sugar   Brown sugar   What is the difference?

. . . .

. . . .

. . . .

Is there a difference if warm water is used?   Yes/No

What is the difference?

. . . .

. . . .

. . . .

Think and do

How does stirring help?

Try it and see.

Drinking chocolate

 ## Read

William had a drink of hot chocolate before going to sleep.
There was a little chocolate left in the cup. By morning it had 'dried up'.

 ## What to do

What has happened to the liquid?

. . . .

What has happened to the chocolate in the drink?

. . . .

 William washes out the cup with warm water.

What happens to the chocolate?

. . . .

. . . .

. . . .

 ## Think and do

On the side of the tin of drinking chocolate it said it contained:

Food colour	Chocolate powder
Flavour	Sugar

←

What happens to all these things when the drink is made?

. . . .

What happens to the Smarties?

Investigate

Add one red Smartie to a glass of water. Do not stir.
Watch and draw what happens.

To another glass of water, add two different coloured Smarties.
Watch and draw what happens.

Think and do

What do you think will happen when you try with other coloured Smarties?

Try it and see.

© Alan Jones, Roy Purnell & Janet O'Neill This sheet may be photocopied for use by the purchasing institution only.

Tea bags

Read

A **filter** separates insoluble materials from liquids.

What to do

A tea bag has tea leaves inside a thin bag with small holes in it.
Draw how the colour and taste of the tea soaks through the bag.

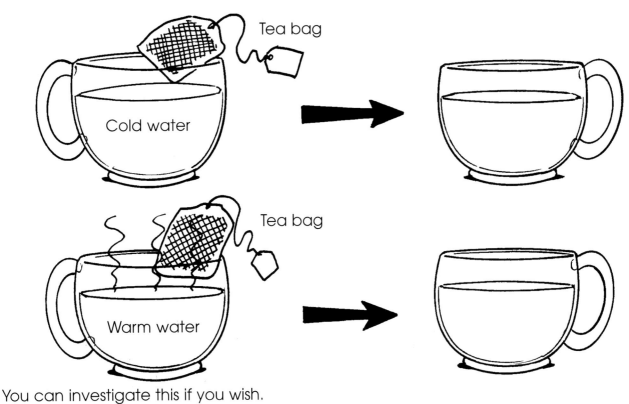

Tea bag

Cold water

Tea bag

Warm water

You can investigate this if you wish.

Think and do

What things in the tea bag are soluble in water? . . . .

. . . .

What things are insoluble? . . . .

. . . .

What difference does it make using warm water? . . . .

. . . .

The material in the tea bag is a food f _ _ _ _ _ .

Filtering

What to do

Razina makes coffee from powdered coffee beans and boiling water.

Paper cone

Chose the correct word to finish each sentence:

filters   **residue**   **dissolves**

The paper cone . . . . the soluble coffee from the beans.

The insoluble material left on the paper is called the . . . .

Part of the coffee bean . . . . and passes through the cone to give the flavour and taste.

Think and do

What is meant by **filtering**?

. . . .

. . . .

Changes

Read

Some changes are easily **reversed** (changed back). Some are not.

What to do

Are these changes easily reversed?   Write **Yes** or **No**.

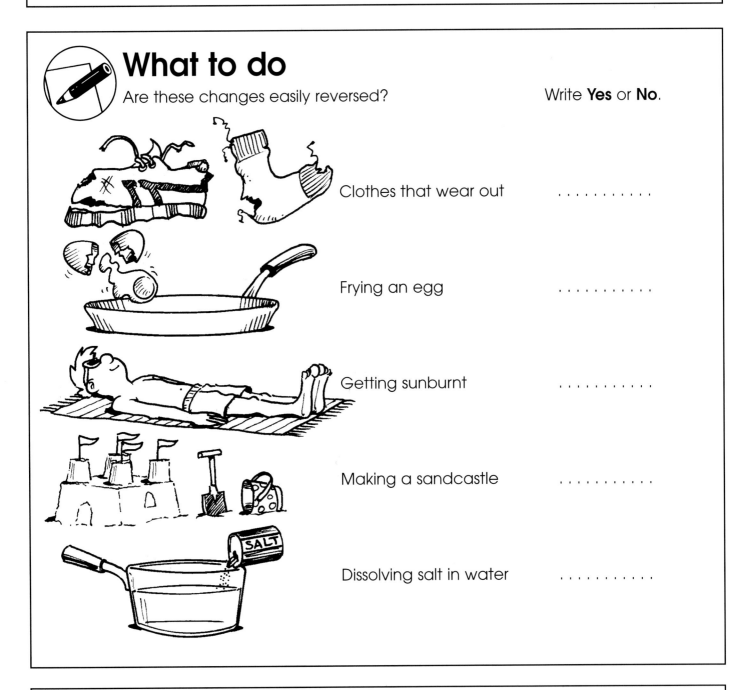

Clothes that wear out   . . . .

Frying an egg   . . . .

Getting sunburnt   . . . .

Making a sandcastle   . . . .

Dissolving salt in water   . . . .

Think and do

Reversible changes can be changed back to where you started.
Non-reversible changes cannot be changed back.

Do you think eating food is reversible?   Yes/No

What to do

For breakfast Joe has a piece of toast.

Finish the drawing to show how toast is different from bread.

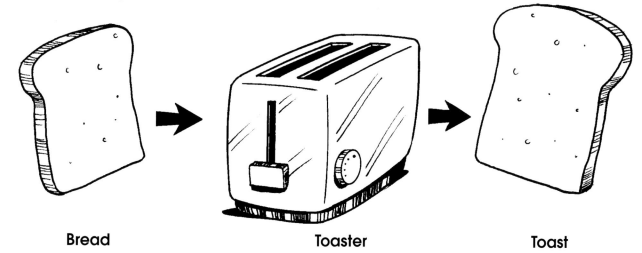

Bread   **Toaster**   **Toast**

Can you turn the toast back into bread?   Yes/No

Draw what happens if a piece of fresh bread is left open to the air for a few weeks.

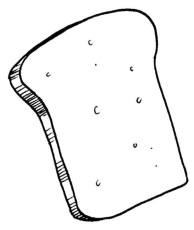

Bread before   Bread after

Can you change these things back?   Yes/No

Think and do

Are the changes that happen to the bread reversible or non-reversible?

. . . .

Changes to a flame

Investigate

Try this investigation.

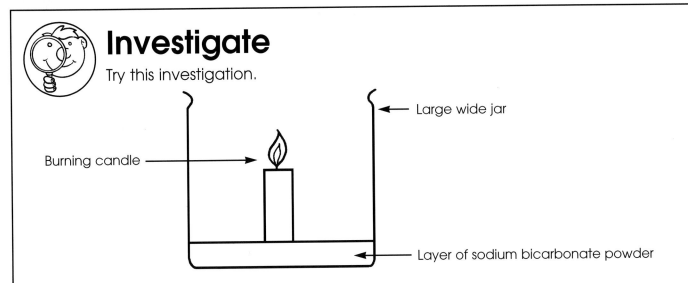

Large wide jar

Burning candle

Layer of sodium bicarbonate powder

Add one spoonful of vinegar.

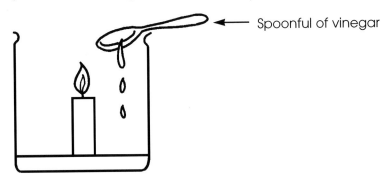

Spoonful of vinegar

The sodium bicarbonate and vinegar fizz and give off carbon dioxide gas.

Draw what happens.

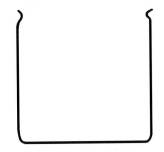

List things that changed:

. . . .

. . . .

. . . .

Think and do

What use could vinegar and sodium bicarbonate be put to?

. . . .

This sheet may be photocopied for use by the purchasing institution only.

What to do

Write what happens to the things in each picture.

Cold drink

What happens to the ice?

. . . .

What happens to the water?

. . . .

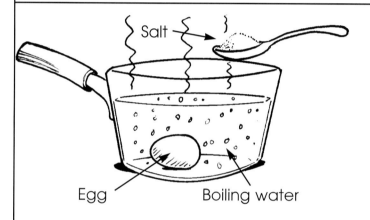

Salt

Egg   Boiling water

What happens to the salt?

. . . .

What happens to the boiling water?

. . . .

What happens to the egg?

. . . .

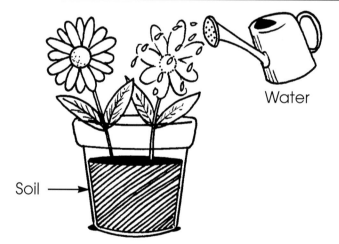

Water

Soil

What happens to the water?

. . . .

. . . .

Think and do

Look at the pictures again.
Find two non-reversible changes that are happening.

. . . .

Burning a candle

What to do

Your teacher will light a candle. Watch it burning from a safe distance.

Draw lines from the labels to the diagram.

Pool of melted wax

Wick of candle

Yellow flame

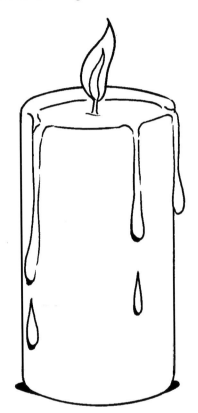

Hot air above flame

Melted wax going solid down sides

Write or draw what happens when the flame is put out.

Think and do

Cut up these sentences and put them in order of what you saw.

The wick was lit by the match.
The candle wax melted.
The match was lit.
The candle burned with a yellow flame.

What is in the bubbles?

Investigate

Half fill a bottle with water. Screw on the top. Shake for one minute. Draw what you see.

Water

Shake bottle

Are there any bubbles?

. . . .

Half fill a bottle with water. Add one drop of washing-up liquid. Screw on the top. Shake for one minute. Draw what you see.

Washing-up liquid

Water

Shake bottle

How long do the bubbles last?

. . . .

What do you think is inside the bubbles?

. . . .

. . . .

Think and do

What could you add to the water to make the bubbles burst?

 Salt  Sugar  Soap  A few drops of vinegar

Try the investigation before answering.

What is needed?

What to do

Put ticks ✓ to show what is needed by each of the following things.
(Some might need more than one tick.)

	Air	Water	Light	Food
Flower in pot				
Burning candle				
Cat				
Flying kite				
Fish				
Camera				
Tree				
Worm				

Think and do

Which of these things do you need?

☐ Air   ☐ Water   ☐ Light   ☐ Food

Why? . . . .

Compost

 Read

Compost-making is a slow, non-reversible change.
The materials change slowly into new, different ones.

What to do

Put a tick ✓ by the materials that you think will make good compost.

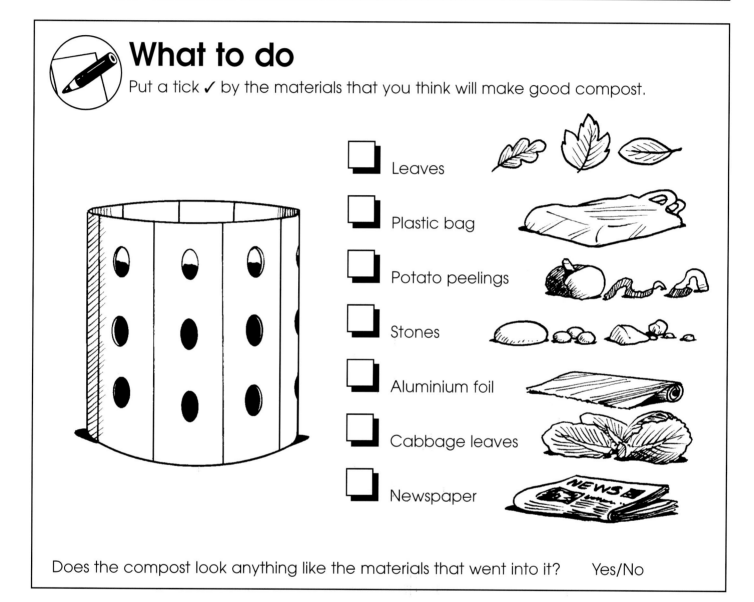

☐ Leaves

☐ Plastic bag

☐ Potato peelings

☐ Stones

☐ Aluminium foil

☐ Cabbage leaves

☐ Newspaper

Does the compost look anything like the materials that went into it?   Yes/No

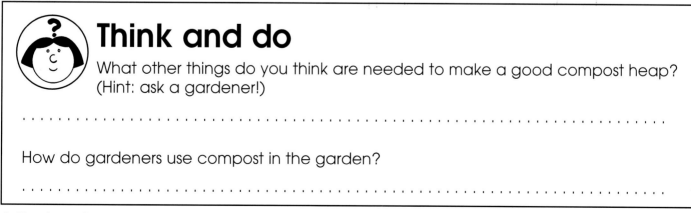 **Think and do**

What other things do you think are needed to make a good compost heap?
(Hint: ask a gardener!)

. . . .

How do gardeners use compost in the garden?

. . . .

Water cycle

 ## What to do

Kelly notices that, at bath-time, the cold windows get all 'steamed up'. Why?

The windows get 'steamed up' because:

. . . .

. . . .

In the winter Jack noticed that his bedroom windows are wet. Why?

The windows are wet because:

. . . .

. . . .

 ## Think and do

Write or draw how you think rain-clouds are formed.

What happens?

What to do

Write what happens in each picture.

Lucy adds salt and potatoes to boiling water.

What happens to the potatoes?

. . . .

Which is soluble in water, salt or potatoes?

. . . .

Ravi waters a plant.

What happens to the water?

. . . .

Claire hangs wet washing on the line. It is windy.

What happens to the water?

. . . .

Sam uses a paper towel to mop up water.

What happens to the water?

. . . .

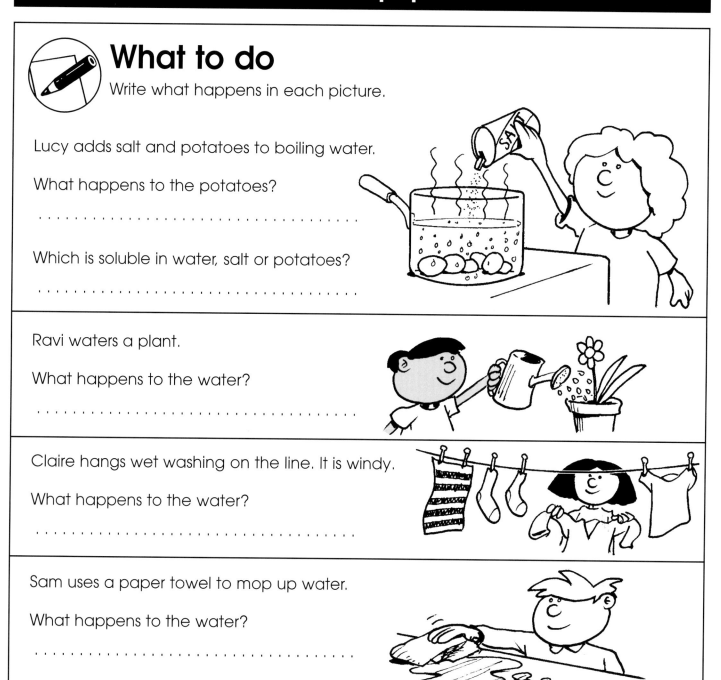

Think and do

Write or draw what you think happens to water when it goes down the plughole.

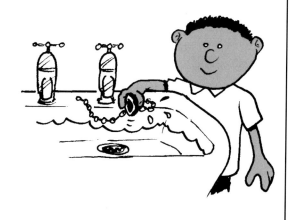

Snowman

 ## Read

Jo and Di built a big
snowman one winter.

 ## What to do

The next morning the snowman had got smaller and it had icicles hanging
from its nose and fingers. The scarf had gone all stiff.

What must have happened to the temperature
overnight?

. . . .

. . . .

. . . .

 ## Think and do

Draw what the snowman would look like if the sun came out.

Where does the snow go? . . . .

. . . .

Jelly and plaster

Read

Different materials have different properties.

What to do

Paul has a plaster cast on his arm. He is eating jelly.
Draw lines from some of the words to label the plaster cast and the jelly.

Hard

Soft

Made by mixing
with water

See-through

Not see-through

Sets quickly

Sets hard

Sets wobbly

Think and do

Why do you think Paul's cast was
made of plaster and not jelly?

. . . .

. . . .

The lost ring

Read

Sophie and Mark's mother has lost her wedding ring on the beach. Sophie and Mark help her to find it using their fishing net.

This beach has so much sand and so many stones. How am I going to find my ring?

We'll help you!

What to do

Draw or write to show what you think they did.

1. First they …	2. Then they …
3. Then …	4. At last! …

Think and do

Can you think of two other ways to find the ring?

. . . .

. . . .

How much will disolve?

Read

There is a limit to how much of a material will dissolve in water.
Different things dissolve in different amounts.

Investigate

Add one spoonful of sugar to a cup of warm water. Stir.
Will it dissolve?   Yes/No

Keep adding sugar, one spoonful at a time, until no more dissolves.
Count how many spoonfuls you add.

I added . . . . spoonfuls of sugar until no more would dissolve in the water.

Now try the same investigation with salt.

1, 2, 3 . . .

I added . . . . spoonfuls of salt until no more would dissolve in the water.
Which is the most soluble, salt or sugar? . . . .

Think and do

Do you think the same amount of sugar and salt would dissolve in cold water?

. . . .

Concrete

 ## What to do

Andy was helping his dad to lay a concrete path.

These are the materials they used to make the concrete:

| Sand | Water | Pebbles | Cement |

Draw or write some instructions for them:

1. First …	2. Then …
3. Then …	4. Lastly …

 ## Think and do

Give three ways that concrete is different from the materials it is made from.

1. ....

2. ....

3. ....

What other things can concrete be used for?

Hot and cold

What to do

Draw lines from the cups of liquids to the thermometers.

Tap water

100ºC

0ºC

Iced water

100ºC

0ºC

Hot tea

100ºC

0ºC

Think and do

About what temperature would this thermometer read if it was placed under your arm?

60ºC
50
40
30
20
10
0

How hot has an oven got to be to cook a cake?

50ºC   100ºC   50ºC   200ºC

Gases in liquids

What to do

What are the gas bubbles in lemonade?

Put a tick ✓ or a cross ✗.

Air ☐

Carbon dioxide ☐

Oxygen ☐

When you buy a can of lemonade you buy the liquid, the can and the gas, which is dissolved in the lemonade.

What happens to the gas?..

At the end of the drink you have separated the solid . . . .

from the liquid . . . .

and the bubbles of . . . .

Think and do

Read and copy out what is written on the side of a can of cola about what is in it.

What to do

Write or draw how you could help to solve these problems.

A sailor is stranded on a desert island. He wants to make drinking water from sea water. How can the sailor do it?

. . . .

. . . .

. . . .

. . . .

 A farmer digs a well in his field. He wants fresh water, but the water has some small bits of dirt in it. How can he purify (clean) the water?

. . . .

. . . .

. . . .

. . . .

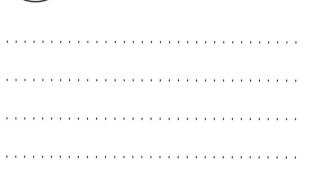

 An engineer wants to find out if there are any iron girders in a wall of a house. She doesn't want to damage the wall. How can she find out?

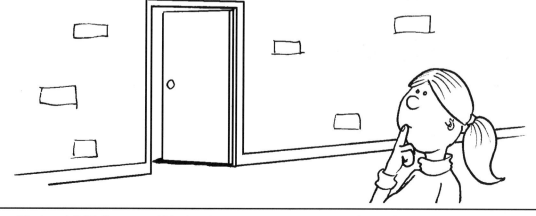

This sheet may be photocopied for use by the purchasing institution only.

What to do

Look at the diagram. Work out a way to make the water level
a) fall. ↓
b) rise. ↑

Write or draw your answers.

. . . .

. . . .

. . . .

. . . .

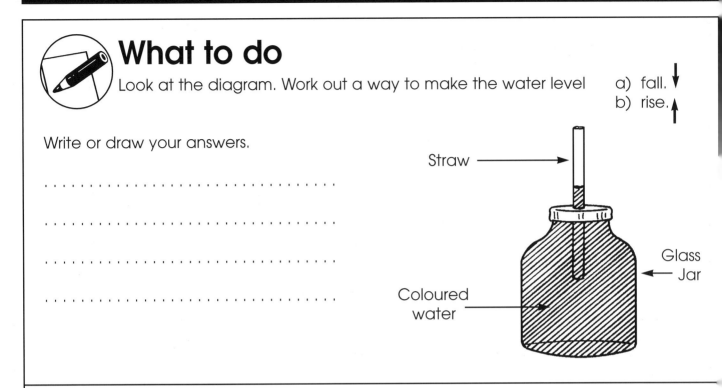

Straw

Glass
Jar

Coloured
water

Look at the diagram. Write or draw what will happen to the wooden stick if
the wire is heated.

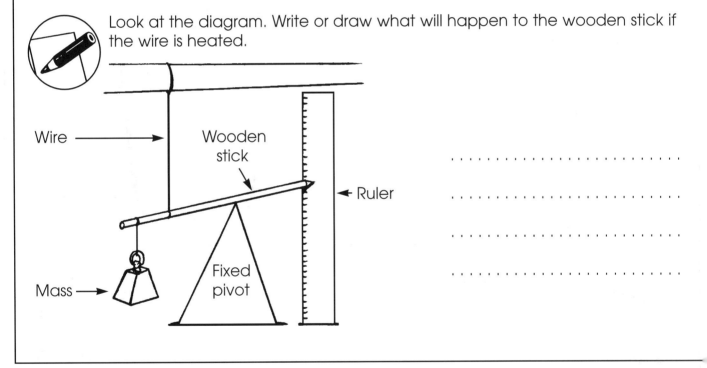

Wire

Wooden
stick

Ruler

Mass

Fixed
pivot

. . . .

. . . .

. . . .

. . . .

Think and do

What could the instruments in the pictures above be used to measure?

How would you go about doing this?

. . . .

. . . .

What to do
Look at the results of this experiment. Write and explain what has happened.

The candle has gone out because ...

. . . .

. . . .

. . . .

. . . .

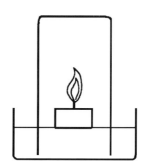 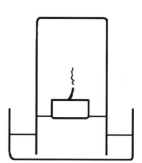

 What will happen to the water level as the ice cubes melt?

The water level will ...

. . . .

. . . .

. . . .

. . . .

 What will happen to the balance as the ice cubes melt?

The balance will ...

. . . .

. . . .

. . . .

. . . .

Problem solving, 4

 ## What to do

Look at the results of this investigation.

Dry air

1

Air

2

Wet
cotton wool

Water
(no air)

3

Tightly screwed
jam jars and
shiny nails.

The nail in Jar 2 went rusty.
Can you explain why?

. . . .

. . . .

 On a cold winter's morning there are droplets of water on the inside of the
bedroom window.

Where have they come from?

. . . .

. . . .

 Look at this picture.

What has caused the gate to go rusty?

. . . .

Brick wall   Rusty gate   Limestone wall

The limestone wall and the brick
wall were built at the same time.
Why has the limestone wall worn
away more?

. . . .

© Alan Jones, Roy Purnell & Janet O'Neill